50 A Taste of Thailand Recipes for Home

By: Kelly Johnson

Table of Contents

- Tom Yum Goong (Spicy Shrimp Soup)
- Pad Thai (Stir-Fried Noodles)
- Green Curry Chicken
- Massaman Curry
- Som Tum (Papaya Salad)
- Tom Kha Gai (Coconut Chicken Soup)
- Pad Krapow Moo (Basil Pork Stir-Fry)
- Larb Gai (Spicy Chicken Salad)
- Panang Curry
- Thai Fried Rice
- Red Curry Duck
- Moo Pad Krapow (Basil Beef)
- Gaeng Garee (Yellow Curry)
- Nam Tok (Waterfall Beef Salad)
- Pad See Ew (Stir-Fried Noodles with Soy Sauce)
- Satay Chicken Skewers
- Khao Soi (Coconut Curry Noodle Soup)
- Pla Rad Prik (Crispy Fish with Chili Sauce)
- Shrimp Toast
- Thai Spring Rolls
- Coconut Sticky Rice with Mango
- Pad Woon Sen (Stir-Fried Glass Noodles)
- Gaeng Phed (Red Curry)
- Thai Beef Salad
- Khai Jiew (Thai Omelette)
- Moo Yang (Grilled Pork)
- Massaman Curry with Beef
- Spicy Thai Noodle Salad
- Thai Iced Tea
- Curry Puffs
- Thai Basil Chicken
- Coconut Soup with Tofu
- Grilled Eggplant Salad
- Thai Green Papaya Salad
- Pineapple Fried Rice

- Sweet and Sour Chicken
- Fish Sauce Wings
- Red Curry with Vegetables
- Thai Cucumber Salad
- Thai Chili Jam
- Coconut Curry Shrimp
- Grilled Pork Skewers with Peanut Sauce
- Stir-Fried Morning Glory
- Tamarind Fish
- Thai Prawn Cakes
- Beef Satay with Peanut Sauce
- Vegetable Spring Rolls
- Thai Mango Salad
- Thai Hot and Sour Soup
- Coconut Pandan Cake

Tom Yum Goong (Spicy Shrimp Soup)

Ingredients:

- 1 lb shrimp, peeled and deveined
- 4 cups chicken broth
- 2 stalks lemongrass, chopped
- 3-4 kaffir lime leaves
- 3-4 slices galangal (or ginger)
- 3-4 Thai bird chilies, smashed
- 200g mushrooms, sliced
- Fish sauce and lime juice, to taste
- Fresh cilantro, for garnish

Instructions:

1. In a pot, bring chicken broth to a boil; add lemongrass, lime leaves, galangal, and chilies.
2. Simmer for 5-10 minutes, then add shrimp and mushrooms.
3. Cook until shrimp is pink, then season with fish sauce and lime juice. Garnish with cilantro.

Pad Thai (Stir-Fried Noodles)

Ingredients:

- 8 oz rice noodles
- 1/2 cup tofu or shrimp
- 2 eggs, beaten
- 1 cup bean sprouts
- 1/4 cup peanuts, crushed
- 3 tbsp fish sauce
- 1 tbsp tamarind paste
- 2 tbsp sugar
- Green onions and lime wedges, for serving

Instructions:

1. Cook noodles according to package instructions; drain.
2. In a pan, heat oil and fry tofu or shrimp until cooked. Push to the side and scramble eggs.
3. Add noodles, fish sauce, tamarind, sugar, and bean sprouts; stir-fry until combined. Serve topped with peanuts, green onions, and lime.

Green Curry Chicken

Ingredients:

- 1 lb chicken, sliced
- 1 can coconut milk
- 3 tbsp green curry paste
- 1 cup eggplant, diced
- 1 bell pepper, sliced
- Fresh basil, for garnish

Instructions:

1. In a pot, heat coconut milk and add green curry paste; stir until combined.
2. Add chicken and cook until browned, then add eggplant and bell pepper.
3. Simmer until vegetables are tender. Garnish with fresh basil.

Massaman Curry

Ingredients:

- 1 lb beef or chicken, cubed
- 1 can coconut milk
- 3 tbsp massaman curry paste
- 2 potatoes, diced
- 1 onion, chopped
- 1/4 cup peanuts

Instructions:

1. In a pot, heat coconut milk and curry paste until fragrant.
2. Add meat and cook until browned, then add potatoes and onion.
3. Simmer until meat is tender and potatoes are cooked; stir in peanuts before serving.

Som Tum (Papaya Salad)

Ingredients:

- 2 cups shredded green papaya
- 1 carrot, shredded
- 2-3 Thai bird chilies, smashed
- 2 tbsp fish sauce
- 1 tbsp lime juice
- 1/4 cup peanuts, crushed

Instructions:

1. In a bowl, combine papaya, carrot, chilies, fish sauce, and lime juice.
2. Toss well and top with crushed peanuts before serving.

Tom Kha Gai (Coconut Chicken Soup)

Ingredients:

- 1 lb chicken, sliced
- 4 cups coconut milk
- 2 stalks lemongrass, chopped
- 3-4 kaffir lime leaves
- 3-4 slices galangal (or ginger)
- 200g mushrooms, sliced
- Fish sauce and lime juice, to taste
- Fresh cilantro, for garnish

Instructions:

1. In a pot, bring coconut milk to a simmer; add lemongrass, lime leaves, and galangal.
2. Add chicken and mushrooms, cooking until chicken is done. Season with fish sauce and lime juice. Garnish with cilantro.

Pad Krapow Moo (Basil Pork Stir-Fry)

Ingredients:

- 1 lb ground pork
- 4 cloves garlic, minced
- 2-3 Thai bird chilies, chopped
- 2 tbsp soy sauce
- 1 tbsp fish sauce
- 1 cup Thai basil leaves

Instructions:

1. In a pan, sauté garlic and chilies until fragrant.
2. Add ground pork and cook until browned; stir in soy sauce and fish sauce.
3. Add basil leaves just before serving; serve hot with rice.

Larb Gai (Spicy Chicken Salad)

Ingredients:

- 1 lb ground chicken
- 1/4 cup lime juice
- 2-3 Thai bird chilies, chopped
- 1/4 cup fish sauce
- 1/2 cup fresh mint leaves
- 1/2 cup fresh cilantro

Instructions:

1. Cook ground chicken in a pan until browned; remove from heat.
2. In a bowl, mix lime juice, chilies, fish sauce, mint, cilantro, and chicken.
3. Serve with lettuce leaves for wrapping.

Enjoy your cooking!

Panang Curry

Ingredients:

- 1 lb chicken or beef, sliced
- 1 can coconut milk
- 3 tbsp Panang curry paste
- 1 red bell pepper, sliced
- Fresh basil, for garnish

Instructions:

1. In a pot, heat coconut milk and stir in curry paste until fragrant.
2. Add meat and cook until browned; then add bell pepper and simmer until tender.
3. Garnish with fresh basil before serving.

Thai Fried Rice

Ingredients:

- 2 cups cooked jasmine rice
- 1/2 cup cooked chicken, shrimp, or tofu
- 2 eggs, beaten
- 1 cup mixed vegetables (carrots, peas, corn)
- 3 tbsp soy sauce
- Green onions, for garnish

Instructions:

1. In a wok, scramble the eggs and set aside.
2. Stir-fry chicken or shrimp until cooked, then add vegetables and rice.
3. Add soy sauce and scrambled eggs; toss to combine. Garnish with green onions.

Red Curry Duck

Ingredients:

- 1 lb duck breast, sliced
- 1 can coconut milk
- 3 tbsp red curry paste
- 1 cup bamboo shoots
- Fresh basil, for garnish

Instructions:

1. In a pan, heat coconut milk and stir in red curry paste until aromatic.
2. Add duck and cook until browned; then add bamboo shoots and simmer.
3. Garnish with fresh basil before serving.

Moo Pad Krapow (Basil Beef)

Ingredients:

- 1 lb ground beef
- 4 cloves garlic, minced
- 2-3 Thai bird chilies, chopped
- 2 tbsp soy sauce
- 1 tbsp fish sauce
- 1 cup Thai basil leaves

Instructions:

1. In a pan, sauté garlic and chilies until fragrant.
2. Add ground beef and cook until browned; stir in soy sauce and fish sauce.
3. Fold in basil leaves just before serving; serve with rice.

Gaeng Garee (Yellow Curry)

Ingredients:

- 1 lb chicken or tofu, cubed
- 1 can coconut milk
- 3 tbsp yellow curry paste
- 2 potatoes, diced
- 1 onion, chopped

Instructions:

1. In a pot, heat coconut milk and stir in yellow curry paste.
2. Add chicken or tofu, potatoes, and onion; simmer until cooked through.

Nam Tok (Waterfall Beef Salad)

Ingredients:

- 1 lb grilled beef, sliced
- 1/4 cup lime juice
- 2-3 Thai bird chilies, chopped
- 1/4 cup fish sauce
- 1/2 cup fresh mint and cilantro

Instructions:

1. In a bowl, combine lime juice, chilies, fish sauce, and beef; toss well.
2. Add mint and cilantro before serving.

Pad See Ew (Stir-Fried Noodles with Soy Sauce)

Ingredients:

- 8 oz wide rice noodles
- 1 lb chicken or pork, sliced
- 2 cups broccoli or Chinese broccoli
- 2 eggs, beaten
- 3 tbsp soy sauce
- 1 tbsp oyster sauce

Instructions:

1. Cook noodles according to package instructions; drain.
2. In a wok, stir-fry meat until cooked, then add broccoli and stir-fry for a few minutes.
3. Push ingredients to the side, scramble eggs, then add noodles and sauces; toss to combine.

Satay Chicken Skewers

Ingredients:

- 1 lb chicken breast, cut into strips
- 1/4 cup peanut butter
- 2 tbsp soy sauce
- 1 tbsp curry powder
- Skewers

Instructions:

1. In a bowl, mix peanut butter, soy sauce, and curry powder.
2. Marinate chicken strips in the mixture for at least 30 minutes.
3. Thread onto skewers and grill until cooked through; serve with peanut sauce if desired.

Enjoy your cooking!

Khao Soi (Coconut Curry Noodle Soup)

Ingredients:

- 8 oz egg noodles
- 1 lb chicken or beef, sliced
- 1 can coconut milk
- 3 tbsp red curry paste
- 4 cups chicken broth
- Lime wedges and cilantro, for garnish

Instructions:

1. Cook noodles according to package instructions; set aside.
2. In a pot, heat coconut milk and curry paste; add meat and cook until browned.
3. Pour in chicken broth and simmer; serve over noodles, garnished with lime and cilantro.

Pla Rad Prik (Crispy Fish with Chili Sauce)

Ingredients:

- 1 whole fish, cleaned
- 1/2 cup cornstarch
- Oil, for frying
- 1/4 cup chili sauce
- 1/4 cup onion, sliced
- 1/4 cup bell pepper, sliced

Instructions:

1. Dust the fish with cornstarch. Heat oil in a pan and fry until crispy; drain.
2. In another pan, sauté onion and bell pepper, then add chili sauce.
3. Pour the sauce over the crispy fish before serving.

Shrimp Toast

Ingredients:

- 1 lb shrimp, peeled and deveined
- 1/4 cup scallions, chopped
- 1 egg, beaten
- 4 slices white bread
- Sesame seeds, for topping
- Oil, for frying

Instructions:

1. Blend shrimp, scallions, and egg into a paste.
2. Spread on bread slices and sprinkle with sesame seeds.
3. Fry in hot oil until golden brown; drain before serving.

Thai Spring Rolls

Ingredients:

- 8 spring roll wrappers
- 1 cup mixed vegetables (carrots, cabbage, bean sprouts)
- 1/2 cup cooked shrimp or tofu (optional)
- Oil, for frying

Instructions:

1. Place a small amount of filling on each wrapper and roll tightly, sealing edges with water.
2. Fry in hot oil until golden; drain on paper towels.

Coconut Sticky Rice with Mango

Ingredients:

- 1 cup sticky rice
- 1 can coconut milk
- 1/4 cup sugar
- 1 ripe mango, sliced

Instructions:

1. Soak sticky rice for at least 2 hours; steam until cooked.
2. In a pan, heat coconut milk with sugar until dissolved.
3. Serve sticky rice drizzled with coconut milk and topped with mango.

Pad Woon Sen (Stir-Fried Glass Noodles)

Ingredients:

- 8 oz glass noodles
- 1 lb chicken or shrimp, sliced
- 2 cups mixed vegetables (carrots, bell peppers)
- 2 eggs, beaten
- 3 tbsp soy sauce
- 1 tbsp oyster sauce

Instructions:

1. Soak glass noodles in hot water until soft; drain.
2. In a wok, stir-fry meat until cooked, then add vegetables and cook for a few minutes.
3. Push to the side, scramble eggs, then add noodles and sauces; toss to combine.

Gaeng Phed (Red Curry)

Ingredients:

- 1 lb chicken or tofu, cubed
- 1 can coconut milk
- 3 tbsp red curry paste
- 1 cup eggplant, diced
- Fresh basil, for garnish

Instructions:

1. In a pot, heat coconut milk and stir in red curry paste until fragrant.
2. Add meat and eggplant; simmer until cooked. Garnish with fresh basil before serving.

Thai Beef Salad

Ingredients:

- 1 lb grilled beef, sliced
- 1/4 cup lime juice
- 2-3 Thai bird chilies, chopped
- 1/4 cup fish sauce
- 2 cups mixed greens

Instructions:

1. In a bowl, combine lime juice, chilies, fish sauce, and beef; toss well.
2. Serve over mixed greens.

Enjoy your cooking!

Khai Jiew (Thai Omelette)

Ingredients:

- 4 eggs
- 2 tbsp fish sauce
- 1 green onion, chopped
- Oil, for frying

Instructions:

1. Beat eggs with fish sauce and green onion.
2. Heat oil in a pan and pour in the egg mixture, cooking until set and golden brown.
3. Flip to cook both sides and serve hot.

Moo Yang (Grilled Pork)

Ingredients:

- 1 lb pork shoulder, sliced thin
- 1/4 cup soy sauce
- 2 tbsp sugar
- 2 tbsp fish sauce
- 3 cloves garlic, minced
- Skewers

Instructions:

1. Marinate pork in soy sauce, sugar, fish sauce, and garlic for at least 1 hour.
2. Thread onto skewers and grill until cooked through.

Massaman Curry with Beef

Ingredients:

- 1 lb beef, cubed
- 1 can coconut milk
- 3 tbsp massaman curry paste
- 2 potatoes, diced
- 1 onion, chopped
- Peanuts, for garnish

Instructions:

1. In a pot, heat coconut milk and curry paste until fragrant.
2. Add beef, potatoes, and onion; simmer until tender.
3. Garnish with peanuts before serving.

Spicy Thai Noodle Salad

Ingredients:

- 8 oz rice noodles
- 1 cup mixed vegetables (carrots, bell peppers)
- 1/4 cup lime juice
- 2 tbsp fish sauce
- 2-3 Thai bird chilies, chopped
- Fresh cilantro, for garnish

Instructions:

1. Cook noodles according to package instructions; drain.
2. Toss noodles with vegetables, lime juice, fish sauce, and chilies.
3. Garnish with cilantro before serving.

Thai Iced Tea

Ingredients:

- 4 cups water
- 4 tbsp Thai tea leaves
- 1/4 cup sugar
- 1/2 cup condensed milk

Instructions:

1. Boil water and steep tea leaves for 5 minutes; strain.
2. Stir in sugar and let cool. Serve over ice with condensed milk.

Curry Puffs

Ingredients:

- 1 cup puff pastry
- 1/2 lb ground chicken or tofu
- 1/4 cup potato, diced
- 1 tbsp curry powder
- Oil, for frying

Instructions:

1. Sauté chicken or tofu with potatoes and curry powder.
2. Roll out pastry, fill with mixture, and seal edges.
3. Fry in hot oil until golden brown.

Thai Basil Chicken

Ingredients:

- 1 lb ground chicken
- 4 cloves garlic, minced
- 2-3 Thai bird chilies, chopped
- 2 tbsp soy sauce
- 1 tbsp fish sauce
- 1 cup Thai basil leaves

Instructions:

1. In a pan, sauté garlic and chilies until fragrant.
2. Add ground chicken and cook until browned; stir in soy and fish sauces.
3. Add basil leaves just before serving; serve with rice.

Coconut Soup with Tofu

Ingredients:

- 1 can coconut milk
- 1 cup vegetable broth
- 1 block tofu, cubed
- 2-3 kaffir lime leaves
- 1 tbsp lime juice
- Fresh cilantro, for garnish

Instructions:

1. In a pot, combine coconut milk and broth; add lime leaves and bring to a simmer.
2. Add tofu and cook until heated through; stir in lime juice.
3. Garnish with cilantro before serving.

Enjoy your cooking!

Grilled Eggplant Salad

Ingredients:

- 2 medium eggplants, sliced
- 2 tbsp fish sauce
- 2 tbsp lime juice
- 1 clove garlic, minced
- 1/4 cup chopped cilantro
- Chili flakes, to taste

Instructions:

1. Grill eggplant slices until tender and charred.
2. In a bowl, mix fish sauce, lime juice, garlic, and chili flakes.
3. Toss grilled eggplant with dressing and garnish with cilantro before serving.

Thai Green Papaya Salad

Ingredients:

- 2 cups green papaya, shredded
- 1 carrot, shredded
- 2-3 Thai bird chilies, chopped
- 3 tbsp fish sauce
- 2 tbsp lime juice
- 1/4 cup peanuts, crushed

Instructions:

1. In a bowl, combine papaya, carrot, and chilies.
2. Mix fish sauce and lime juice; pour over salad and toss.
3. Top with crushed peanuts before serving.

Pineapple Fried Rice

Ingredients:

- 2 cups cooked jasmine rice
- 1 cup pineapple, diced
- 1/2 cup peas and carrots
- 2 eggs, beaten
- 3 tbsp soy sauce
- Green onions, for garnish

Instructions:

1. In a wok, scramble eggs and set aside.
2. Stir-fry rice with pineapple and vegetables; add soy sauce.
3. Fold in scrambled eggs and garnish with green onions.

Sweet and Sour Chicken

Ingredients:

- 1 lb chicken breast, cubed
- 1 cup bell peppers, diced
- 1 cup pineapple chunks
- 1/4 cup ketchup
- 2 tbsp vinegar
- 2 tbsp sugar

Instructions:

1. In a pan, cook chicken until browned; add bell peppers and pineapple.
2. Mix ketchup, vinegar, and sugar; pour over chicken and simmer until thickened.

Fish Sauce Wings

Ingredients:

- 2 lbs chicken wings
- 1/4 cup fish sauce
- 2 tbsp lime juice
- 2 tbsp honey
- 4 cloves garlic, minced

Instructions:

1. Marinate wings in fish sauce, lime juice, honey, and garlic for at least 1 hour.
2. Bake or grill wings until crispy and cooked through.

Red Curry with Vegetables

Ingredients:

- 1 can coconut milk
- 2-3 tbsp red curry paste
- 2 cups mixed vegetables (bell peppers, zucchini, carrots)
- Fresh basil, for garnish

Instructions:

1. In a pot, heat coconut milk and stir in red curry paste.
2. Add vegetables and simmer until tender; garnish with fresh basil.

Thai Cucumber Salad

Ingredients:

- 2 cucumbers, thinly sliced
- 1/4 cup vinegar
- 2 tbsp sugar
- 1/4 cup peanuts, crushed
- Chili flakes, to taste

Instructions:

1. In a bowl, mix vinegar and sugar until dissolved.
2. Add cucumbers and toss; top with crushed peanuts and chili flakes before serving.

Thai Chili Jam

Ingredients:

- 10-12 dried red chilies
- 1/2 cup shallots, sliced
- 2 cloves garlic, minced
- 1/4 cup tamarind paste
- 1/4 cup palm sugar
- 1/4 cup fish sauce

Instructions:

1. Soak dried chilies in hot water until soft; blend with shallots and garlic.
2. In a pan, combine the chili mixture with tamarind paste, palm sugar, and fish sauce; simmer until thickened.

Enjoy your cooking!

Coconut Curry Shrimp

Ingredients:

- 1 lb shrimp, peeled and deveined
- 1 can coconut milk
- 2 tbsp red curry paste
- 1 bell pepper, sliced
- 1 cup snap peas
- Fresh basil, for garnish

Instructions:

1. In a pan, heat coconut milk and stir in red curry paste until fragrant.
2. Add shrimp, bell pepper, and snap peas; simmer until shrimp are cooked through.
3. Garnish with fresh basil before serving.

Grilled Pork Skewers with Peanut Sauce

Ingredients:

- 1 lb pork tenderloin, cut into cubes
- 1/4 cup soy sauce
- 2 tbsp brown sugar
- 2 tbsp fish sauce
- Skewers

Peanut Sauce:

- 1/2 cup peanut butter
- 1/4 cup coconut milk
- 2 tbsp soy sauce
- 1 tbsp lime juice

Instructions:

1. Marinate pork in soy sauce, brown sugar, and fish sauce for at least 1 hour.
2. Thread onto skewers and grill until cooked through.
3. For the peanut sauce, whisk together peanut butter, coconut milk, soy sauce, and lime juice. Serve skewers with sauce.

Stir-Fried Morning Glory

Ingredients:

- 1 lb morning glory (water spinach), trimmed
- 4 cloves garlic, minced
- 2 tbsp oyster sauce
- 1 tbsp soy sauce
- 1 tbsp vegetable oil

Instructions:

1. Heat oil in a wok and sauté garlic until fragrant.
2. Add morning glory and stir-fry for 2-3 minutes.
3. Add oyster sauce and soy sauce; stir until well combined.

Tamarind Fish

Ingredients:

- 2 fish fillets (tilapia or snapper)
- 1/4 cup tamarind paste
- 2 tbsp fish sauce
- 1 tbsp sugar
- 1 tbsp lime juice

Instructions:

1. In a bowl, mix tamarind paste, fish sauce, sugar, and lime juice.
2. Marinate fish in the mixture for 15-30 minutes.
3. Bake or grill the fish until cooked through.

Thai Prawn Cakes

Ingredients:

- 1 lb shrimp, peeled and deveined
- 1/4 cup green beans, finely chopped
- 1 egg
- 1 tbsp fish sauce
- 1/2 cup breadcrumbs
- Oil, for frying

Instructions:

1. Pulse shrimp in a food processor until finely chopped; mix with green beans, egg, fish sauce, and breadcrumbs.
2. Form into patties and fry in hot oil until golden brown on both sides.

Beef Satay with Peanut Sauce

Ingredients:

- 1 lb beef, thinly sliced
- 1/4 cup soy sauce
- 2 tbsp curry powder
- 2 tbsp brown sugar
- Skewers

Peanut Sauce:

- 1/2 cup peanut butter
- 1/4 cup coconut milk
- 1 tbsp soy sauce
- 1 tbsp lime juice

Instructions:

1. Marinate beef in soy sauce, curry powder, and brown sugar for at least 1 hour.
2. Thread onto skewers and grill until cooked through.
3. For the peanut sauce, whisk together peanut butter, coconut milk, soy sauce, and lime juice. Serve with satay.

Vegetable Spring Rolls

Ingredients:

- 8 rice paper wrappers
- 1 cup mixed vegetables (carrots, cucumber, bell peppers), julienned
- Fresh herbs (mint, cilantro)
- Dipping sauce (sweet chili sauce or peanut sauce)

Instructions:

1. Soak rice paper wrappers in warm water until pliable.
2. Place vegetables and herbs in the center of each wrapper and roll tightly.
3. Serve with dipping sauce.

Thai Mango Salad

Ingredients:

- 2 ripe mangoes, julienned
- 1 carrot, julienned
- 1/4 cup red onion, thinly sliced
- 1/4 cup cilantro, chopped
- 2 tbsp lime juice
- 2 tbsp fish sauce
- 1 tbsp sugar

Instructions:

1. In a bowl, combine mangoes, carrot, red onion, and cilantro.
2. In a separate bowl, whisk together lime juice, fish sauce, and sugar; pour over salad and toss to combine.

Enjoy your cooking!

Thai Hot and Sour Soup (Tom Yum)

Ingredients:

- 4 cups chicken or vegetable broth
- 1 stalk lemongrass, cut into 2-inch pieces and smashed
- 3-4 kaffir lime leaves
- 3-4 slices galangal (or ginger)
- 200g shrimp or chicken, sliced
- 1 cup mushrooms, sliced
- 2-3 Thai bird chilies, smashed (adjust for heat)
- 3 tbsp fish sauce
- 1 tbsp lime juice
- Fresh cilantro, for garnish

Instructions:

1. In a pot, bring broth to a boil and add lemongrass, kaffir lime leaves, and galangal.
2. Simmer for 5-10 minutes to infuse flavors.
3. Add shrimp (or chicken) and mushrooms; cook until shrimp are pink and chicken is cooked through.
4. Stir in bird chilies, fish sauce, and lime juice.
5. Remove from heat and garnish with fresh cilantro before serving.

Coconut Pandan Cake

Ingredients:

- 1 cup all-purpose flour
- 1 cup coconut milk
- 1 cup sugar
- 1/2 cup pandan juice (blend pandan leaves with water and strain)
- 4 eggs
- 1/2 cup vegetable oil
- 2 tsp baking powder
- 1/4 tsp salt

Instructions:

1. Preheat the oven to 350°F (175°C). Grease a cake pan.
2. In a bowl, mix flour, baking powder, and salt.
3. In another bowl, whisk eggs and sugar until light and fluffy.
4. Gradually add coconut milk, pandan juice, and vegetable oil; mix until well combined.
5. Slowly fold in the dry ingredients until just combined.
6. Pour the batter into the prepared pan and bake for 30-35 minutes or until a toothpick comes out clean.
7. Let cool before slicing and serving.

Enjoy your cooking!

www.ingramcontent.com/pod-product-compliance
Lightning Source LLC
LaVergne TN
LVHW061953070526
838199LV00060B/4087